This book is printed in the United States of America by Joy K. Blair., No material contained in this book may be copied or retrieved in any manner for sale, but may be used in teaching and instruction for the body of Christ.

Photograph by Ed Carpenter

ISBN- 978-1470067991
Printed in the United States of America

Copyright ©2012 by Joy K. Blair

Joy K. Blair
P. O. Box 303
Florissant MO 63032

Joysready34@yahoo.com

This Book Belongs To:

_____

From:

_____

Date:

_____

FASTING IS THE KEY

21 DAY DEVOTIONAL

Joy Blair

Introduction

Fasting is a very powerful tool, especially in the hands of believers. When you implement fasting with God's word and prayer things must change, doors must open, demons are defeated and territory is enlarged. Through fasting, a twisted and distorted view of life is overthrown and life through the eyes of God takes on its rightful perspective. God is so faithful and true. He has a remedy in His word for everything that we go through. Right now your remedy is fasting and meditating on the word of God. Understand that this is not a onetime event but a lifelong discipline. If you are willing and obedient every time God calls you to fast, you will inherit the land of whatever is on the other side of your fast. Whenever God calls you on a fast, it's for a purpose, it's a warfare tactic and strategy for victory, your enemy is on the loose and out to destroy you. Fasting will help you to overcome the temptations that are set to alter and destroy your times and seasons. As you get closer to your purpose, the traps are so much more luring and deceptive. Fasting humbles you so the things that your flesh usually craves, will not seem so irresistible. You'll have a spiritual point of view instead of a worldly point of view which includes the lust of the flesh, lust of the eyes and the pride of life. As you take the sword of the spirit which is the word of God and apply it with fasting and prayer, your life will change forever. The power of God rests on a consecrated life. God wants to do great things through you, but you must get out of His way and fasting is the key to less of you and more of God. In this 21 day fast, God is going to turn your life around. Let's read what Joel 2:12-26 say's about fasting and the benefits that comes with it;

"Therefore also now, saith the LORD, turn ye even to me with all your heart, and with fasting, and with weeping, and with mourning: And rend your heart, and not your garments, and turn unto the LORD your God: for he is gracious and merciful, slow to anger, and of great kindness, and repenteth him of the evil. Who knoweth if he will return and repent, and leave a blessing behind him; even a meat offering and a drink offering unto the LORD your God? Blow the trumpet in Zion, sanctify a fast, call a solemn assembly: Gather the people, sanctify the congregation, assemble the elders, gather the children, and those that suck the breasts: let the bridegroom go forth of his chamber, and the bride out of her closet. Let the priests, the ministers of the LORD, weep between the porch and the altar, and let them say, Spare thy people, O LORD, and give not thine heritage to reproach, that the heathen should rule over them: wherefore should they say among the people, Where is their God? Then will the LORD be jealous for his land, and pity his people. Yea, the LORD will answer and say unto his people, Behold, I will send you corn, and wine, and oil, and ye shall be satisfied therewith: and I will no more make you a reproach among the heathen: But I will remove far off from you the northern army, and will drive him into a land barren and desolate, with his face toward the east sea, and his hinder part toward the utmost sea, and his stink shall come up, and his ill savour shall come up, because he hath done great things. Fear not, O land; be glad and rejoice: for the LORD will do great things. Be not afraid, ye beasts of the field: for the pastures of the wilderness do spring, for the tree beareth her fruit, the fig tree and the vine do yield their strength. Be glad then, ye children of Zion, and rejoice in the LORD your God: for he hath given you the former rain moderately, and he will cause to come down for you the rain, the former rain, and the latter rain in the first month. And the floors shall be full of wheat, and the vats shall overflow with wine and oil. And I will restore to you the years that the locust hath eaten, the cankerworm, and the caterpiller, and the palmerworm, my great army which I sent among you. And ye shall eat in plenty, and be satisfied, and praise the name of the LORD your God, that hath dealt wondrously with you: and my people shall never be ashamed".

God said in Deuteronomy 8:3 that He led you all this way through the wilderness to humble you so that you will know that man does not live by bread alone but by every word that proceeds out of the mouth of God. Fasting is like going through a wilderness, but in your low and dry places, you'll learn the true value of God's word and how important it is in order to thrive as a believer in Jesus Christ. We are to work out our own salvation with fear and trembling. Fasting is the key to overcoming you.

FASTING

IS

THE KEY

21 DAY DEVOTIONAL

Day One

LORD HELP ME

Sometimes life can get so tough that it seems so hard to pray, but during those times, you must press in even harder. When you don't know the words to say, just open your mouth and say "Lord, help me". God will hear your prayer and answer your plea. Thank God that when we don't know what to pray, the Holy Spirit makes intercession for us. When you feel as if you are not worthy to pray to God, just repent and by faith cry out with all your heart. The reason you are in prayer mode is because God is drawing you closer to Him. Accept His divine invitation today. He is calling you closer and closer to Him. He wants an intimate relationship with you. He wants to change you from the inside out. He wants to purge and purify you. He wants to enlarge your territory. He has a great plan in store for you. It's not too late to start a new chapter in your life. Open your heart and allow God to come in and sweep you clean. He will give you a new heart and renew the right spirit within you. Trust Him today to help you. Let it all go, everything that is a hindrance to your relationship with God. This fast is designed to take you to a new level in Christ Jesus.

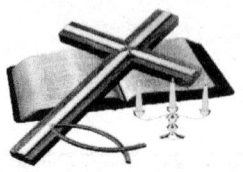

Deuteronomy 1:1-18

These be the words which Moses spake unto all Israel on this side Jordan in the wilderness, in the plain over against the Red sea, between Paran, and Tophel, and Laban, and Hazeroth, and Dizahab. (There are eleven days' journey from Horeb by the way of mount Seir unto Kadeshbarnea.) And it came to pass in the fortieth year, in the eleventh month, on the first day of the month, that Moses spake unto the children of Israel, according unto all that the LORD had given him in commandment unto them; After he had slain Sihon the king of the Amorites, which dwelt in Heshbon, and Og the king of Bashan, which dwelt at Astaroth in Edrei: On this side Jordan, in the land of Moab, began Moses to declare this law, saying, The LORD our God spake unto us in Horeb, saying, Ye have dwelt long enough in this mount: Turn you, and take your journey, and go to the mount of the Amorites, and unto all the places nigh thereunto, in the plain, in the hills, and in the vale, and in the south, and by the sea side, to the land of the Canaanites, and unto Lebanon, unto the great river, the river Euphrates. Behold, I have set the land before you: go in and possess the land which the LORD sware unto your fathers, Abraham, Isaac, and Jacob, to give unto them and to their seed after them. And I spake unto you at that time, saying, I am not able to bear you myself alone: The LORD your God hath multiplied you, and, behold, ye are this day as the stars of heaven for multitude. (The LORD God of your fathers make you a thousand times so many more as ye are, and bless you, as he hath promised you!) How can I myself alone bear your cumbrance, and your burden, and your strife? Take you wise men, and understanding, and known among your tribes, and I will make them rulers over you. And ye answered me, and said, The thing which thou hast spoken is good for us to do. So I took the chief of your tribes, wise men, and known, and made them heads over you, captains over thousands, and captains over hundreds, and captains over fifties, and captains over tens, and officers among your tribes. And I charged your judges at that time, saying, Hear the causes between your brethren, and judge righteously between every man and his brother, and the stranger that is with him. Ye shall not respect persons in judgment; but ye shall hear the small as well as the great; ye shall not be afraid of the face of man; for the judgment is God's: and the cause that is too hard for you, bring it unto me, and I will hear it. And I commanded you at that time all the things which ye should do.

Notes_____

_____

_____

_____

_____

_____

Day Two

WHEN THE ENEMY COMES IN LIKE A FLOOD

The Bible says; So shall they fear the name of the LORD from the west, and his glory from the rising of the sun. When the enemy shall come in like a flood, the Spirit of the LORD shall lift up a standard against him. (Isaiah 59:19). God knows all and He sees all. He will not allow the pressure to mount up beyond what you are able to handle, but He has a standard and will not tolerate the devil to cross over it. There is nothing happening to you that God is not aware of. Even in all your pain, suffering and temptations, God is still working it all out for your good. Trust and believe that there is nothing too hard for God. God has called you on this fast because He knows that this kind does not come out except through prayer and fasting. He loves you and cares deeply about every area of your life. Seek God for guidance and ask Him to order your steps. Don't look back any more. Your past is over and your future is waiting. Hold your head up and let God shape you into His image. This chapter of your life is designed to purge away all impurities and cleanse you from ungodliness. Open the eyes and ears of your heart and listen carefully to God's directions and follow His leading.

 **Psalm 46:1-11**

God is our refuge and strength, a very present help in trouble. Therefore will not we fear, though the earth be removed, and though the mountains be carried into the midst of the sea; Though the waters thereof roar and be troubled, though the mountains shake with the swelling thereof. Selah. There is a river, the streams whereof shall make glad the city of God, the holy place of the tabernacles of the most High. God is in the midst of her; she shall not be moved: God shall help her, and that right early. The heathen raged, the kingdoms were moved: he uttered his voice, the earth melted. The LORD of hosts is with us; the God of Jacob is our refuge. Selah. Come, behold the works of the LORD, what desolations he hath made in the earth. He maketh wars to cease unto the end of the earth; he breaketh the bow, and cutteth the spear in sunder; he burneth the chariot in the fire. Be still, and know that I am God: I will be exalted among the heathen, I will be exalted in the earth. The LORD of hosts is with us; the God of Jacob is our refuge. Selah.

Notes

Day Three

SEEKING GOD WITH YOUR WHOLE HEART

God desires and commands that you love Him with your whole heart. He does not want half of you but all of you. He will not share you with the love of this world, for all that's in this world is passing away, the lust of the eyes, the lust of the flesh and the pride of life, will all be destroyed one day. Fasting helps you to humble yourself. It helps to humble your flesh and its lustful desires for the things of this world. In God's presence is fullness of joy and I know you want to be in the presence of the LORD, but it will take some sacrifice. Many people are not willing to sacrifice but they want the anointing and power of God on their lives. The Bible tells us to enter into His presence with thanksgiving and into His courts with praise. Thanksgiving is a sacrifice, fasting is a sacrifice and it's a sweet smelling aroma in the nostrils of God. Commit to living a sacrificed life unto God. Be determined to be loyal and faithful to God. Dedicate your whole heart and life to Him daily and watch the private time you spend with God reward you openly.

Psalm 100:1-5

Make a joyful noise unto the LORD, all ye lands. Serve the LORD with gladness: come before his presence with singing. Know ye that the LORD he is God: it is he that hath made us, and not we ourselves; we are his people, and the sheep of his pasture. Enter into his gates with thanksgiving, and into his courts with praise: be thankful unto him, and bless his name. For the LORD is good; his mercy is everlasting; and his truth endureth to all generations.

Notes_____

_____

_____

_____

_____

_____

_____

Day Four

PUT ON THE WHOLE ARMOR OF GOD

Though you are in the battle and the heat is turned up, God is fighting for you. This heated battle belongs to Him. Position yourself by putting on the whole armor of God that ye may be able to stand against the wiles of the devil. For we wrestle not against flesh and blood, but against principalities, against powers, against the rulers of the darkness of this world, against spiritual wickedness in high places. Wherefore take unto you the whole armor of God that ye may be able to withstand in the evil day, and having done all, to stand. As you stand with the whole armor of God on, stand therefore, having your loins girt about with truth, and having on the breastplate of righteousness; and your feet shod with the preparation of the gospel of peace; above all, taking the shield of faith, wherewith ye shall be able to quench all the fiery darts of the wicked. And take the helmet of salvation, and the sword of the Spirit, which is the word of God: Praying always with all prayer and supplication in the Spirit, and watching thereunto with all perseverance. Finally, be strong in the Lord, and in the power of his might (Ephesians 6:1-18). You can of yourself do nothing but you can leap through troops with God.

Romans 6:1-14

What shall we say then? Shall we continue in sin, that grace may abound? God forbid. How shall we, that are dead to sin, live any longer therein? Know ye not, that so many of us as were baptized into Jesus Christ were baptized into his death? Therefore we are buried with him by baptism into death: that like as Christ was raised up from the dead by the glory of the Father, even so we also should walk in newness of life. For if we have been planted together in the likeness of his death, we shall be also in the likeness of his resurrection: Knowing this, that our old man is crucified with him, that the body of sin might be destroyed, that henceforth we should not serve sin. For he that is dead is freed from sin. Now if we be dead with Christ, we believe that we shall also live with him: Knowing that Christ being raised from the dead dieth no more; death hath no more dominion over him. For in that he died, he died unto sin once: but in that he liveth, he liveth unto God. Likewise reckon ye also yourselves to be dead indeed unto sin, but alive unto God through Jesus Christ our Lord. Let not sin therefore reign in your mortal body, that ye should obey it in the lusts thereof. Neither yield ye your members as instruments of unrighteousness unto sin: but yield yourselves unto God, as those that are alive from the dead, and your members as instruments of righteousness unto God. For sin shall not have dominion over you: for ye are not under the law, but under grace.

Notes

Day Five

THE LORD WILL DELIVER YOU

There is nothing in life that catches God off guard. God knows the beginning, the middle and the very end. He is the creator of all heaven and earth, surely your situations and circumstances are not too hard for Him to handle. Cast all the cares of your heart on Jesus today and trust Him to work it all out for your good. As you fast, it will help you to direct your focus on God and His will for your life and to take your eyes off of yourself. You will soon see just how little your plans are compared to the plans that God has for your life. God has so much in store for you and what you are going through now is just part of the preparation process. You must keep your mind stayed on Jesus and hold on with your very being. Read your Bible daily in order to build your faith. Faith comes by hearing and hearing by the word of God (Romans 10:17). The more you hear the word of God the stronger your faith becomes and the clearer your deliverance will appear.

Psalm 143:1-12

Hear my prayer, O LORD, give ear to my supplications: in thy faithfulness answer me, and in thy righteousness. And enter not into judgment with thy servant: for in thy sight shall no man living be justified. For the enemy hath persecuted my soul; he hath smitten my life down to the ground; he hath made me to dwell in darkness, as those that have been long dead. Therefore is my spirit overwhelmed within me; my heart within me is desolate. I remember the days of old; I meditate on all thy works; I muse on the work of thy hands. I stretch forth my hands unto thee: my soul thirsteth after thee, as a thirsty land. Selah. Hear me speedily, O LORD: my spirit faileth: hide not thy face from me, lest I be like unto them that go down into the pit. Cause me to hear thy lovingkindness in the morning; for in thee do I trust: cause me to know the way wherein I should walk; for I lift up my soul unto thee. Deliver me, O LORD, from mine enemies: I flee unto thee to hide me. Teach me to do thy will; for thou art my God: thy spirit is good; lead me into the land of uprightness. Quicken me, O LORD, for thy name's sake: for thy righteousness' sake bring my soul out of trouble. And of thy mercy cut off mine enemies, and destroy all them that afflict my soul: for I am thy servant.

Notes_____

Day Six

TRUST THE LORD WITH ALL YOUR HEART

Begin this day and every day of your life trusting and relying totally on God for His help, strength, direction, joy, peace, love, encouragement, confidence and simply put, for everything. He is your source. Do not put your trust in no one but God. Allow Him to order your steps and guide you to your safe haven daily. That's why it is so important to live a lifestyle of fasting and praying, because sometimes we tend to get in our own way trying to do God's job. Even though, over a course of life's experiences, we finally realize that we just can't take on the role of God, it's simply too big. Fasting is so vital to our spiritual growth and our physical breakthroughs, that's why we must make it a lifestyle. If you are ready for change, then fasting is a tool that will bring great manifestation into your life. Fasting also helps to put us in our proper and rightful place, on our knees and not on the throne. The only person that should be on the throne of our hearts is Jesus. Purpose in your heart to trust God and to be committed to Him forever, regardless of what the problem is. Trust Him even more when there is blessing all around because after all, all good and perfect gifts come from God. If you allow your success to cause you to be lifted up in pride, you'll soon lose but if you practice fasting, you'll remain humble and gain greater levels of prosperity.

 Proverbs 3:1-6

My son, forget not my law; but let thine heart keep my commandments: For length of days, and long life, and peace, shall they add to thee. Let not mercy and truth forsake thee: bind them about thy neck; write them upon the table of thine heart: So shalt thou find favour and good understanding in the sight of God and man. Trust in the LORD with all thine heart; and lean not unto thine own understanding. In all thy ways acknowledge him, and he shall direct thy paths.

Notes_____

_____

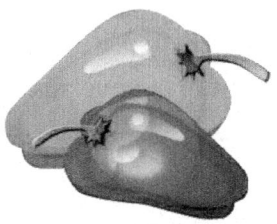

Day Seven

GOD'S WORD WILL NOT RETURN VOID

It is so good to sit silently in the presence of the Lord. So many people are so busy with life that they hardly ever take time out to just sit at the feet of Jesus to listen to what He has to say. One word from the Lord would change your life forever. There's a story in the Bible where Jesus was invited to a lady named Martha's house. She had a sister called Mary who sat at the feet of Jesus as He taught His disciples. Martha was very frustrated because her sister was listening diligently to the words of Jesus and not helping her serve, so she said to Him, "Lord, do You not care that my sister is not helping me serve? Jesus replied to her, "Martha, Martha, you are troubled about many things, but one thing is needed and Mary has chosen that good part" (Luke 10:38-42). In the presence of the Lord waiting patiently for Him to speak is the good part. Reading and meditating on His word is the good part. Fasting and praying is the good part. The more you seek Him, the easier it will be to recognize His voice and as you search the scriptures, you'll learn to believe and receive by faith every promise in His word.

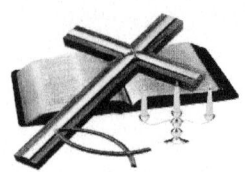

Isaiah 55:1-13

Ho, every one that thirsteth, come ye to the waters, and he that hath no money; come ye, buy, and eat; yea, come, buy wine and milk without money and without price. Wherefore do ye spend money for that which is not bread? and your labour for that which satisfieth not? hearken diligently unto me, and eat ye that which is good, and let your soul delight itself in fatness. Incline your ear, and come unto me: hear, and your soul shall live; and I will make an everlasting covenant with you, even the sure mercies of David. Behold, I have given him for a witness to the people, a leader and commander to the people. Behold, thou shalt call a nation that thou knowest not, and nations that knew not thee shall run unto thee because of the LORD thy God, and for the Holy One of Israel; for he hath glorified thee. Seek ye the LORD while he may be found, call ye upon him while he is near: Let the wicked forsake his way, and the unrighteous man his thoughts: and let him return unto the LORD, and he will have mercy upon him; and to our God, for he will abundantly pardon. For my thoughts are not your thoughts, neither are your ways my ways, saith the LORD. For as the heavens are higher than the earth, so are my ways higher than your ways, and my thoughts than your thoughts. For as the rain cometh down, and the snow from heaven, and returneth not thither, but watereth the earth, and maketh it bring forth and bud, that it may give seed to the sower, and bread to the eater: So shall my word be that goeth forth out of my mouth: it shall not return unto me void, but it shall accomplish that which I please, and it shall prosper in the thing whereto I sent it. For ye shall go out with joy, and be led forth with peace: the mountains and the hills shall break forth before you into singing, and all the trees of the field shall clap their hands. Instead of the thorn shall come up the fir tree, and instead of the brier shall come up the myrtle tree: and it shall be to the LORD for a name, for an everlasting sign that shall not be cut off.

Notes_____

Day Eight

PURSUE THE KNOWLEDGE OF THE LORD

If you have a desire to be successful in any area of your life, it begins with the knowledge of God. As you seek to know the Lord, He will reveal Himself to you through His word. Ask, and it shall be given you; seek, and ye shall find; knock, and it shall be opened unto you (Matthew 7:7). The word of the Lord will enlighten your path. God has all wisdom and knowledge and will open up your eyes of understanding as you seek to draw closer to Him through fasting and studying the Word of God. As you search out the scriptures, you'll gain a new perspective on life, because you will see things as they really are and not for what it appears to be. As you press in to know the Lord, He will strengthen you and prepare you for greatness. During this fast, ask God to give you the desire to study the Word of God. Ask Him to give you spiritual understanding. Ask Him to take away your desire for the things of this world and give you the desires of Jesus. The love of this world will destroy your relationship with the Father. You can't love God and this world, because the Bible tells us that we can't have two masters because we will love one and hate the other. In order to gain Christ, you must forsake all and follow after Him with your whole heart. Fasting helps you to see the vanity in the things this world has to offer us.

Hosea 6:1-3

Come, and let us return unto the LORD: for he hath torn, and he will heal us; he hath smitten, and he will bind us up. After two days will he revive us: in the third day he will raise us up, and we shall live in his sight. Then shall we know, if we follow on to know the LORD: his going forth is prepared as the morning; and he shall come unto us as the rain, as the latter and former rain unto the earth.

Notes

Day Nine

LESS OF ME AND MORE OF HIM

My daily prayer is for more of God and less of me until there is none of me and all of Him. I want to live a life that is full of God. I want to please Him throughout my stay here on earth. I have a fear to leave here with my work undone and the only way I can accomplish my purpose is to deny myself, pick up my cross daily and follow after Him with all my being. Though this seems to be hard to do, fasting helps to rid me of the distractions of this world and it demands focus for the things of God. God wants our lives to exemplify him totally. He does not want us to love this world nor the things of this world more than the love of God. It's time for you to get out of your own way, stop blaming others for your mistakes, take responsibility for your actions, words and laziness, forgive yourself, let go of your past and press on because your destiny awaits. The more time you spend in the word of God, wisdom will permeate throughout your spirit and awaken you to greater levels of integrity. You'll be able to walk upright with a Godly character and help others to do the same.

John 3:27-36

John answered and said, A man can receive nothing, except it be given him from heaven. Ye yourselves bear me witness, that I said, I am not the Christ, but that I am sent before him. He that hath the bride is the bridegroom: but the friend of the bridegroom, which standeth and heareth him, rejoiceth greatly because of the bridegroom's voice: this my joy therefore is fulfilled. He must increase, but I must decrease. He that cometh from above is above all: he that is of the earth is earthly, and speaketh of the earth: he that cometh from heaven is above all. And what he hath seen and heard, that he testifieth; and no man receiveth his testimony. He that hath received his testimony hath set to his seal that God is true. For he whom God hath sent speaketh the words of God: for God giveth not the Spirit by measure unto him. The Father loveth the Son, and hath given all things into his hand. He that believeth on the Son hath everlasting life: and he that believeth not the Son shall not see life; but the wrath of God abideth on him.

Notes_____

Day Ten

DO NOT FEAR YOU WILL NOT BE ASHAMED

You have been through so much in your life time, but believe me God is working on something wonderful for you. God will compensate you for your suffering especially if you are suffering for Christ's name sake. You have to believe that God has a great plan for your life and never give up or lose hope. While you are going through, it is very important to meditate on God's word because it is your hope and it increases your faith. If you have the faith the size of a mustard seed, you will see your dreams come to pass. You'll begin to dream big and do things you've never thought possible. The word of God builds up a strong image on the inside of you. It will take the limits off of you and cause you to think and do mighty works for God. You'll be able to stand full of joy while you are conquering your strongholds and possessing your land that God has promised you. You don't have to be afraid because God is with you and He has already given you all things that pertain to life and godliness. You are fully equipped and ready to be all that God has created you to become.

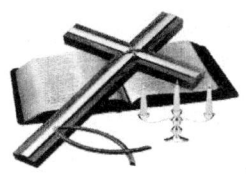

Joshua 1:1-9

Now after the death of Moses the servant of the LORD it came to pass, that the LORD spake unto Joshua the son of Nun, Moses' minister, saying, Moses my servant is dead; now therefore arise, go over this Jordan, thou, and all this people, unto the land which I do give to them, even to the children of Israel. Every place that the sole of your foot shall tread upon, that have I given unto you, as I said unto Moses. From the wilderness and this Lebanon even unto the great river, the river Euphrates, all the land of the Hittites, and unto the great sea toward the going down of the sun, shall be your coast. There shall not any man be able to stand before thee all the days of thy life: as I was with Moses, so I will be with thee: I will not fail thee, nor forsake thee. Be strong and of a good courage: for unto this people shalt thou divide for an inheritance the land, which I sware unto their fathers to give them. Only be thou strong and very courageous, that thou mayest observe to do according to all the law, which Moses my servant commanded thee: turn not from it to the right hand or to the left, that thou mayest prosper withersoever thou goest. This book of the law shall not depart out of thy mouth; but thou shalt meditate therein day and night, that thou mayest observe to do according to all that is written therein: for then thou shalt make thy way prosperous, and then thou shalt have good success. Have not I commanded thee? Be strong and of a good courage; be not afraid, neither be thou dismayed: for the LORD thy God is with thee whithersoever thou goest.

Notes

Day Eleven

GOD MAKE ME OVER

David cried out to God and said, "Create in me a clean heart oh God, and renew the right spirit within me". David was a man after God's own heart, but he had flaws and needed to be made over. Though he loved God, he had fallen into adultery because of covetousness. He saw a beautiful woman and regardless of the fact that she was married, he took her, had sex with her and after she had become pregnant, he tried to frame her husband so that he would think the child was his. David's plan backfired, so he had her husband killed and took her for himself. Yea, sometimes we do things that we are so ashamed of and never want to think on again, but that's when we need to cry out to God for a new heart and a new mind. We can of ourselves do nothing but make a big mess. From the beginning of creation, man began making messes that only God could clean up. Adam and Eve understood this all too well and their mess was passed down to all generations. God had a plan that included us all. God's fix it plan, is passed down to all generations as well, but it's up to us to accept the redemptive plan of God. Our cry daily should be the same as David's, "Create in me a clean heart of God", and renew the right spirit within me". Please Lord, make me over.

Jeremiah 18:1-6

The word which came to Jeremiah from the LORD, saying, Arise, and go down to the potter's house, and there I will cause thee to hear my words. Then I went down to the potter's house, and, behold, he wrought a work on the wheels. And the vessel that he made of clay was marred in the hand of the potter: so he made it again another vessel, as seemed good to the potter to make it. Then the word of the LORD came to me, saying, O house of Israel, cannot I do with you as this potter? saith the LORD. Behold, as the clay is in the potter's hand, so are ye in mine hand, O house of Israel.

Notes_____

Day Twelve

I AM BLESSED AND HIGHLY FAVORED

Change is on the way. Prepare yourself by renewing your mind to the fact that you are blessed and highly favored. In order to receive increase in any area of your life, you must be exposed to a greater level of thinking. Don't look at where you are but vision yourself without limitations. You are more than your current situation. You are an overcomer and created in the image of God, you must think and see yourself that way regardless of the limits around you. My mother always tell me that trouble don't last always. Listen when I tell you that no weapon formed against you shall ever prosper. You are coming out of this and though this battle stinks, you'll have a sweet smell of victory. Though the battle is heated and you are armed and in position, you will not break a nail, because God is fighting this battle for you. He chose to fight it before you were created. He brought you to this place for His names sake and He will get the glory and you will come out with substance and will not leave empty handed. God brought the children of Israel from Egypt to the Red Sea through the wilderness and all He required of them was just to believe that they were blessed and highly favored. When they came up against all their enemies, God gave them instructions and as they obeyed by faith all their enemies were defeated. The only way you'll lose is if you doubt God. You will win and not lose, you are the head and not the tail, you are more than a conqueror and not defeated. If God be for you, who can stand against you in any battle? Nobody, no devil, no enemy, you win, only believe.

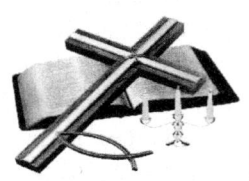

Deuteronomy 28:1-14

And it shall come to pass, if thou shalt hearken diligently unto the voice of the LORD thy God, to observe and to do all his commandments which I command thee this day, that the LORD thy God will set thee on high above all nations of the earth: And all these blessings shall come on thee, and overtake thee, if thou shalt hearken unto the voice of the LORD thy God. Blessed shalt thou be in the city, and blessed shalt thou be in the field. Blessed shall be the fruit of thy body, and the fruit of thy ground, and the fruit of thy cattle, the increase of thy kine, and the flocks of thy sheep. Blessed shall be thy basket and thy store. Blessed shalt thou be when thou comest in, and blessed shalt thou be when thou goest out. The LORD shall cause thine enemies that rise up against thee to be smitten before thy face: they shall come out against thee one way, and flee before thee seven ways. The LORD shall command the blessing upon thee in thy storehouses, and in all that thou settest thine hand unto; and he shall bless thee in the land which the LORD thy God giveth thee. The LORD shall establish thee an holy people unto himself, as he hath sworn unto thee, if thou shalt keep the commandments of the LORD thy God, and walk in his ways. And all people of the earth shall see that thou art called by the name of the LORD; and they shall be afraid of thee. And the LORD shall make thee plenteous in goods, in the fruit of thy body, and in the fruit of thy cattle, and in the fruit of thy ground, in the land which the LORD sware unto thy fathers to give thee. The LORD shall open unto thee his good treasure, the heaven to give the rain unto thy land in his season, and to bless all the work of thine hand: and thou shalt lend unto many nations, and thou shalt not borrow. And the LORD shall make thee the head, and not the tail; and thou shalt be above only, and thou shalt not be beneath; if that thou hearken unto the commandments of the LORD thy God, which I command thee this day, to observe and to do them: And thou shalt not go aside from any of the words which I command thee this day, to the right hand, or to the left, to go after other gods to serve them.

Notes_____
_____
_____
_____
_____
_____
_____
_____

Day Thirteen

I HAVE THE WISDOM OF GOD

Deuteronomy 4:4-6 says "Behold, I have taught you statutes and judgments, even as the LORD my God commanded me that ye should do so in the land whither ye go to possess it. Keep therefore and do them; for this is your wisdom and your understanding in the sight of the nations, which shall hear all these statutes, and say, surely this great nation is a wise and understanding people". Our wisdom is found in God's word. As you spend time in the word of God, you'll gain more than the finest things, or money that perishes, you'll gain and retain life, knowledge, understanding, hope, joy, peace, love and a fruitful life beyond your imagination. Hide the word of God in your heart and cherish it as your greatest prize possession and watch your hidden treasure flourish. The word of God will make you wiser than the most prominent men and women that's living today or that ever lived. I know you desire more in your lifetime then just a normal life. You want your inheritance. You want to walk out the purpose of God and His divine plan for you. Solomon asked God for wisdom and it pleased God so that God gave him riches, honor and so much more. He's still the person that people relate to when they hear the word *"wisdom"*. Seek God and gain wisdom. When Daniel, in the Bible, purposed in his heart to stay pure and holy by fasting, God gave Him wisdom, knowledge and interpretation of dreams and as you fast and purpose in your heart not to defile yourself with this worlds delicacies, God will bless you with a spirit of wisdom to.

Proverbs 8: 6-35

Hear; for I will speak of excellent things; and the opening of my lips shall be right things. For my mouth shall speak truth; and wickedness is an abomination to my lips. All the words of my mouth are in righteousness; there is nothing froward or perverse in them. They are all plain to him that understandeth, and right to them that find knowledge. Receive my instruction, and not silver; and knowledge rather than choice gold. For wisdom is better than rubies; and all the things that may be desired are not to be compared to it. I wisdom dwell with prudence, and find out knowledge of witty inventions. The fear of the LORD is to hate evil: pride, and arrogancy, and the evil way, and the froward mouth, do I hate. Counsel is mine, and sound wisdom: I am understanding; I have strength. By me kings reign, and princes decree justice. By me princes rule, and nobles, even all the judges of the earth. I love them that love me; and those that seek me early shall find me. Riches and honour are with me; yea, durable riches and righteousness. My fruit is better than gold, yea, than fine gold; and my revenue than choice silver. I lead in the way of righteousness, in the midst of the paths of judgment: That I may cause those that love me to inherit substance; and I will fill their treasures. The LORD possessed me in the beginning of his way, before his works of old. I was set up from everlasting, from the beginning, or ever the earth was. When there were no depths, I was brought forth; when there were no fountains abounding with water. Before the mountains were settled, before the hills was I brought forth: While as yet he had not made the earth, nor the fields, nor the highest part of the dust of the world. When he prepared the heavens, I was there: when he set a compass upon the face of the depth: When he established the clouds above: when he strengthened the fountains of the deep: When he gave to the sea his decree, that the waters should not pass his commandment: when he appointed the foundations of the earth: Then I was by him, as one brought up with him: and I was daily his delight, rejoicing always before him; Rejoicing in the habitable part of his earth; and my delights were with the sons of men. Now therefore hearken unto me, O ye children: for blessed are they that keep my ways. Hear instruction, and be wise, and refuse it not. Blessed is the man that heareth me, watching daily at my gates, waiting at the posts of my doors. For whoso findeth me findeth life, and shall obtain favour of the LORD.

Notes_____

_____

_____

Day Fourteen

SPEAK THOSE THINGS

If you keep saying what you see, you'll remain in your same little limited box, your uncomfortable comfort zone. If you are ready for change then you have to call those things that are not as though they are already in existence. If you want a new thing, speak the word of God into the atmosphere. What is God's vision for your life? Are you in agreement with Him? If so then speak what you see. Speak the promises of God every day, over your life. Write down your vision and speak it with conviction. Say it like you mean it. If nobody else believes in you, you must believe in yourself. As you speak the word of God out loud, you are planting seeds and watering your seed, when the season is right, the word of God will sprout up in your life. There is a time and season for everything and when it's your time, there's nothing or no one able to stand in your way. Walk by faith and not by sight. Stay far away from negativity. Separate yourself from anything that's contrary to the word of God. Every ungodly thought that rises up against the word of God, cast is down by declaring what the Bible says. During this fast expect God to give you a new and clear vision of yourself and your life. He is purging and cleansing you for His divine purpose. Pray daily that His will be done in your life.

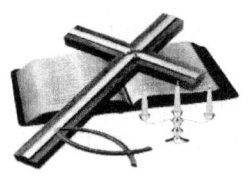

Romans 4:1-21

What shall we say then that Abraham our father, as pertaining to the flesh, hath found? For if Abraham were justified by works, he hath whereof to glory; but not before God. For what saith the scripture? Abraham believed God, and it was counted unto him for righteousness. Now to him that worketh is the reward not reckoned of grace, but of debt. But to him that worketh not, but believeth on him that justifieth the ungodly, his faith is counted for righteousness. Even as David also describeth the blessedness of the man, unto whom God imputeth righteousness without works, Saying, Blessed are they whose iniquities are forgiven, and whose sins are covered. Blessed is the man to whom the Lord will not impute sin. Cometh this blessedness then upon the circumcision only, or upon the uncircumcision also? for we say that faith was reckoned to Abraham for righteousness. How was it then reckoned? when he was in circumcision, or in uncircumcision? Not in circumcision, but in uncircumcision. And he received the sign of circumcision, a seal of the righteousness of the faith which he had yet being uncircumcised: that he might be the father of all them that believe, though they be not circumcised; that righteousness might be imputed unto them also: And the father of circumcision to them who are not of the circumcision only, but who also walk in the steps of that faith of our father Abraham, which he had being yet uncircumcised. For the promise, that he should be the heir of the world, was not to Abraham, or to his seed, through the law, but through the righteousness of faith. For if they which are of the law be heirs, faith is made void, and the promise made of none effect: Because the law worketh wrath: for where no law is, there is no transgression. Therefore it is of faith, that it might be by grace; to the end the promise might be sure to all the seed; not to that only which is of the law, but to that also which is of the faith of Abraham; who is the father of us all, (As it is written, I have made thee a father of many nations,) before him whom he believed, even God, who quickeneth the dead, and calleth those things which be not as though they were. Who against hope believed in hope, that he might become the father of many nations, according to that which was spoken, So shall thy seed be. And being not weak in faith, he considered not his own body now dead, when he was about an hundred years old, neither yet the deadness of Sarah's womb: He staggered not at the promise of God through unbelief; but was strong in faith, giving glory to God; And being fully persuaded that, what he had promised, he was able also to perform.

Notes_____

_____

_____

_____

_____

Day Fifteen

THERE'S NO GREATER LOVE

I know that you have had some failed relationships in your life that has left you broken. God is so faithful and will not leave you in a state of depression but will lift you up from the lowest places in your life and instead of putting those old pieces back together He is doing a new thing. Don't fight with your change anymore. Trust God and know that He has your best interest in mind. God is not like the people that have mistreated you in the past. He is one person that you'll have to never worry about leaving you. Seek God for His guidance and follow Him as he leads you. Estrange yourself from all idols, uncleanness, debauchery, rebellion, fear and anything else that would come to separate you from the will of God. Just take one step at a time toward your future. Make fasting apart of your life and watch God do miracles for you. Pray always and about everything. Do not do anything without God's permission. Put Him first and from this day forward, don't look back but keep your eyes stayed on Jesus, the author and finisher of your faith who kept His eyes on you as He endured the cross, despised the shame and sat down at the right hand of the throne of God.

John 3:1-17

There was a man of the Pharisees, named Nicodemus, a ruler of the Jews: The same came to Jesus by night, and said unto him, Rabbi, we know that thou art a teacher come from God: for no man can do these miracles that thou doest, except God be with him. Jesus answered and said unto him, Verily, verily, I say unto thee, Except a man be born again, he cannot see the kingdom of God. Nicodemus saith unto him, How can a man be born when he is old? can he enter the second time into his mother's womb, and be born? Jesus answered, Verily, verily, I say unto thee, Except a man be born of water and of the Spirit, he cannot enter into the kingdom of God. That which is born of the flesh is flesh; and that which is born of the Spirit is spirit. Marvel not that I said unto thee, Ye must be born again. The wind bloweth where it listeth, and thou hearest the sound thereof, but canst not tell whence it cometh, and whither it goeth: so is every one that is born of the Spirit. Nicodemus answered and said unto him, How can these things be? Jesus answered and said unto him, Art thou a master of Israel, and knowest not these things? Verily, verily, I say unto thee, We speak that we do know, and testify that we have seen; and ye receive not our witness. If I have told you earthly things, and ye believe not, how shall ye believe, if I tell you of heavenly things? And no man hath ascended up to heaven, but he that came down from heaven, even the Son of man which is in heaven. And as Moses lifted up the serpent in the wilderness, even so must the Son of man be lifted up: That whosoever believeth in him should not perish, but have eternal life. For God so loved the world, that he gave his only begotten Son, that whosoever believeth in him should not perish, but have everlasting life. For God sent not his Son into the world to condemn the world; but that the world through him might be saved.

Notes_____

_____
_____
_____
_____
_____
_____
_____
_____
_____
_____
_____
_____
_____
_____

Day Sixteen

LEAVING MY PAST BEHIND

Let no man say when he's tempted that it's God who is tempting Him to do wrong. God can and will not tempt you to sin. He hates and will not tolerate it, so why would He tempt you to return to your old ways. Your past is a place of death and not life. The more you keep looking back to things that can't build you up you stunt your spiritual growth and delay your inheritance. Your past is over and you must let it die and never resurrect it again. Stop talking about it, because the more you talk about it the more you have the opportunity to go backwards. God is wisdom and He only makes wise investments. If you are not mature enough to handle a greater level of blessing, He will not release them to you. You are designed for greatness, but you must desire what's ahead of you more than what's behind you. In the Bible, Jesus warns us about looking back like Lot's wife did when she was told by the angels not to look back. Apparently there was something she felt to be valued back in her past, a place that God delivered her from, and was reluctant to see the plan of God for her future. Her family was told that if they looked back they would turn into a pillow of salt. Lot's wife disobeyed and is still frozen to this day. Looking back paralyzes you and you are not able to move forward. Leave your past behind mentally, emotionally, spiritually and physically. Release yourself to live an abundant life. The devil desires to steal your future by constantly reminding you of your past. Jesus died so that you might have life and have it to the fullest.

Luke 17:20-37

And when he was demanded of the Pharisees, when the kingdom of God should come, he answered them and said, The kingdom of God cometh not with observation: Neither shall they say, Lo here! or, lo there! for, behold, the kingdom of God is within you. And he said unto the disciples, The days will come, when ye shall desire to see one of the days of the Son of man, and ye shall not see it. And they shall say to you, See here; or, see there: go not after them, nor follow them. For as the lightning, that lighteneth out of the one part under heaven, shineth unto the other part under heaven; so shall also the Son of man be in his day. But first must he suffer many things, and be rejected of this generation. And as it was in the days of Noe, so shall it be also in the days of the Son of man. They did eat, they drank, they married wives, they were given in marriage, until the day that Noah entered into the ark, and the flood came, and destroyed them all. Likewise also as it was in the days of Lot; they did eat, they drank, they bought, they sold, they planted, they builded; But the same day that Lot went out of Sodom it rained fire and brimstone from heaven, and destroyed them all. Even thus shall it be in the day when the Son of man is revealed. In that day, he which shall be upon the housetop, and his stuff in the house, let him not come down to take it away: and he that is in the field, let him likewise not return back. Remember Lot's wife. Whosoever shall seek to save his life shall lose it; and whosoever shall lose his life shall preserve it. I tell you, in that night there shall be two men in one bed; the one shall be taken, and the other shall be left. Two women shall be grinding together; the one shall be taken, and the other left. Two men shall be in the field; the one shall be taken, and the other left. And they answered and said unto him, Where, Lord? And he said unto them, Wheresoever the body is, thither will the eagles be gathered together.

Notes_____
_____
_____
_____
_____

Day Seventeen

FAITH TO MOVE FORWARD

Now faith is the substance of things hoped for, the evidence of things not seen. Whenever you are walking by faith, you will always be walking in the *now*. Not tomorrow not yesterday but *now*. Faith is a very exciting place to be because it is a place of hope. Why would a person need to have hope for something they already have? You will only need faith to work for you if you have something you're expecting to come to pass in your life. When you are walking by faith, everything around you will be contrary to what you are hoping for. That's why you must lock into your zone of belief and allow nothing to distract your vision. Build your faith with the word of God by reading, studying, meditating and confessing it constantly until what God has promised you manifest in your life. When you are really in faith, you will be provoked to action for faith without works is dead. Your heart is open to receive the best that God has for you. Listen to His directions and whatever He tells or leads you to do, do it with all your heart and expect Him to do what you can't. Whatever it is, it will be bigger than you, but always remember, it's not by power nor by might but by the Spirit of the Lord. As you humble yourself with fasting, God will lift you up in your due season.

James 2:1-26

My brethren, have not the faith of our Lord Jesus Christ, the Lord of glory, with respect of persons. For if there come unto your assembly a man with a gold ring, in goodly apparel, and there come in also a poor man in vile raiment; And ye have respect to him that weareth the gay clothing, and say unto him, Sit thou here in a good place; and say to the poor, Stand thou there, or sit here under my footstool: Are ye not then partial in yourselves, and are become judges of evil thoughts? Hearken, my beloved brethren, Hath not God chosen the poor of this world rich in faith, and heirs of the kingdom which he hath promised to them that love him? But ye have despised the poor. Do not rich men oppress you, and draw you before the judgment seats? Do not they blaspheme that worthy name by the which ye are called? If ye fulfil the royal law according to the scripture, Thou shalt love thy neighbour as thyself, ye do well: But if ye have respect to persons, ye commit sin, and are convinced of the law as transgressors. For whosoever shall keep the whole law, and yet offend in one point, he is guilty of all. For he that said, Do not commit adultery, said also, Do not kill. Now if thou commit no adultery, yet if thou kill, thou art become a transgressor of the law. So speak ye, and so do, as they that shall be judged by the law of liberty. For he shall have judgment without mercy, that hath shewed no mercy; and mercy rejoiceth against judgment. What doth it profit, my brethren, though a man say he hath faith, and have not works? can faith save him? If a brother or sister be naked, and destitute of daily food, And one of you say unto them, Depart in peace, be ye warmed and filled; notwithstanding ye give them not those things which are needful to the body; what doth it profit? Even so faith, if it hath not works, is dead, being alone. Yea, a man may say, Thou hast faith, and I have works: shew me thy faith without thy works, and I will shew thee my faith by my works. Thou believest that there is one God; thou doest well: the devils also believe, and tremble. But wilt thou know, O vain man, that faith without works is dead? Was not Abraham our father justified by works, when he had offered Isaac his son upon the altar? Seest thou how faith wrought with his works, and by works was faith made perfect? And the scripture was fulfilled which saith, Abraham believed God, and it was imputed unto him for righteousness: and he was called the Friend of God. Ye see then how that by works a man is justified, and not by faith only. Likewise also was not Rahab the harlot justified by works, when she had received the messengers, and had sent them out another way? For as the body without the spirit is dead, so faith without works is dead also.

Notes_____
_____

Day Eighteen

CREATE IN ME A CLEAN HEART

Let us lay aside every sin and weight that so easily ensnares us and let us run the race that is set before us, looking unto Jesus, the Author and Finisher of our faith who for the joy that was set before Him, endured the cross, despised the shame and has set down at the right hand of the throne of God (Hebrews 12:1-2). The hidden secrets and sin of your heart is not worthy to be compared with the glory and favor God has in store for you. You are right at the edge of a major breakthrough, great opportunity for God's kingdom. With the promotion come many adversaries that are designed to launch attacks against you in order to stop you from your purpose in life. Once evil spirits are cast out, they go around in dry places looking for some place to live, when they find no place, they return to their old home to live. The enemy will bring back your old ways, temptations and lusts, but you have the power, which is the word of God to resist the temptations that he offers.

The lust of the heart, the lust of the eyes and the pride of life is how they enter into your soul, once you purpose in your heart to follow Jesus and never to return to your old ways again, they can't stand a chance. The Bible says that some can come out by nothing but fasting and praying, that's why it is so important for you to fill up on the word of God so you'll be able to resist the enemy. God's word is your spiritual food, the more you eat, the stronger you become. Draw close to God, resist the devil and he will flee from you.

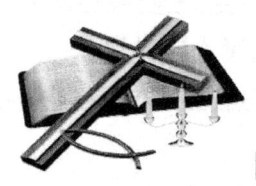

Psalm 51:1-19

Have mercy upon me, O God, according to thy lovingkindness: according unto the multitude of thy tender mercies blot out my transgressions. Wash me throughly from mine iniquity, and cleanse me from my sin. For I acknowledge my transgressions: and my sin is ever before me. Against thee, thee only, have I sinned, and done this evil in thy sight: that thou mightest be justified when thou speakest, and be clear when thou judgest. Behold, I was shapen in iniquity; and in sin did my mother conceive me. Behold, thou desirest truth in the inward parts: and in the hidden part thou shalt make me to know wisdom. Purge me with hyssop, and I shall be clean: wash me, and I shall be whiter than snow. Make me to hear joy and gladness; that the bones which thou hast broken may rejoice. Hide thy face from my sins, and blot out all mine iniquities. Create in me a clean heart, O God; and renew a right spirit within me. Cast me not away from thy presence; and take not thy holy spirit from me. Restore unto me the joy of thy salvation; and uphold me with thy free spirit. Then will I teach transgressors thy ways; and sinners shall be converted unto thee. Deliver me from bloodguiltiness, O God, thou God of my salvation: and my tongue shall sing aloud of thy righteousness. O Lord, open thou my lips; and my mouth shall shew forth thy praise. For thou desirest not sacrifice; else would I give it: thou delightest not in burnt offering. The sacrifices of God are a broken spirit: a broken and a contrite heart, O God, thou wilt not despise. Do good in thy good pleasure unto Zion: build thou the walls of Jerusalem. Then shalt thou be pleased with the sacrifices of righteousness, with burnt offering and whole burnt offering: then shall they offer bullocks upon thine altar.

Notes_____

Day Nineteen

FIRST THINGS FIRST

Putting God first before anything and anyone every day is the key to success. It's a true sign of having no other God's in your life. Spending the first portion of your day with God will bring total peace and balance to a life of chaos. By sacrificing a few minutes of extra sleep to get up and seek the Lord will change your life drastically. God will order your steps, give you favor, open doors that no man could shut because you put Him first. As you pray early in the morning, you will be able to send out your prayers to cover your family, friends, homes, businesses, ministries and everything attached to your life by applying the blood of Jesus covenant for protection from the enemy throughout the day. Your day will go so much smoother because you have aligned your life by putting God first. Fasting shows just how serious you are about doing the will of God. As you fast and pray, casting all your cares on God, you will see Him work your problems out right before your eyes and you will also see your enemy cut off in his place. God will turn your sorrow into joy. Always put God first and watch Him work miracles for you each day.

Matthew 6:19-33

Lay not up for yourselves treasures upon earth, where moth and rust doth corrupt, and where thieves break through and steal: But lay up for yourselves treasures in heaven, where neither moth nor rust doth corrupt, and where thieves do not break through nor steal: For where your treasure is, there will your heart be also. The light of the body is the eye: if therefore thine eye be single, thy whole body shall be full of light. But if thine eye be evil, thy whole body shall be full of darkness. If therefore the light that is in thee be darkness, how great is that darkness! No man can serve two masters: for either he will hate the one, and love the other; or else he will hold to the one, and despise the other. Ye cannot serve God and mammon. Therefore I say unto you, Take no thought for your life, what ye shall eat, or what ye shall drink; nor yet for your body, what ye shall put on. Is not the life more than meat, and the body than raiment? Behold the fowls of the air: for they sow not, neither do they reap, nor gather into barns; yet your heavenly Father feedeth them. Are ye not much better than they? Which of you by taking thought can add one cubit unto his stature? And why take ye thought for raiment? Consider the lilies of the field, how they grow; they toil not, neither do they spin: And yet I say unto you, That even Solomon in all his glory was not arrayed like one of these. Wherefore, if God so clothe the grass of the field, which to day is, and to morrow is cast into the oven, shall he not much more clothe you, O ye of little faith? Therefore take no thought, saying, What shall we eat? or, What shall we drink? or, Wherewithal shall we be clothed? (For after all these things do the Gentiles seek:) for your heavenly Father knoweth that ye have need of all these things. But seek ye first the kingdom of God, and his righteousness; and all these things shall be added unto you.

Notes_____
_____
_____
_____
_____
_____
_____
_____
_____
_____

Day Twenty

ACKNOWLEDGE GOD IN ALL YOUR WAYS

God is doing great things in your life. He is rearranging things and preparing you for your future. With each thought that you think, trust Jesus. With each move that you make, consult God first. Pray to Him about everything and follow as He leads you on the right path of your life. Don't be afraid to take a leap of faith when He directs you to move forward. You will not have to do it alone because God will never leave you, He'll always be there to help you. He has already gone ahead of you to make your crooked paths straight. Keep moving forward taking one step at a time until you reach your destination. Allow God to take you places that you haven't imagined. As long as you follow Jesus, your eyes have not seen, your ears have not heard, nor has your heart ever imagined what God has in store for you.

Romans 8:1-39

There is therefore now no condemnation to them which are in Christ Jesus, who walk not after the flesh, but after the Spirit. For the law of the Spirit of life in Christ Jesus hath made me free from the law of sin and death. For what the law could not do, in that it was weak through the flesh, God sending his own Son in the likeness of sinful flesh, and for sin, condemned sin in the flesh: That the righteousness of the law might be fulfilled in us, who walk not after the flesh, but after the Spirit. For they that are after the flesh do mind the things of the flesh; but they that are after the Spirit the things of the Spirit. For to be carnally minded is death; but to be spiritually minded is life and peace. Because the carnal mind is enmity against God: for it is not subject to the law of God, neither indeed can be. So then they that are in the flesh cannot please God. But ye are not in the flesh, but in the Spirit, if so be that the Spirit of God dwell in you. Now if any man have not the Spirit of Christ, he is none of his. And if Christ be in you, the body is dead because of sin; but the Spirit is life because of righteousness. But if the Spirit of him that raised up Jesus from the dead dwell in you, he that raised up Christ from the dead shall also quicken your mortal bodies by his Spirit that dwelleth in you. Therefore, brethren, we are debtors, not to the flesh, to live after the flesh. For if ye live after the flesh, ye shall die: but if ye through the Spirit do mortify the deeds of the body, ye shall live. For as many as are led by the Spirit of God, they are the sons of God. For ye have not received the spirit of bondage again to fear; but ye have received the Spirit of adoption, whereby we cry, Abba, Father. The Spirit itself beareth witness with our spirit, that we are the children of God: And if children, then heirs; heirs of God, and joint-heirs with Christ; if so be that we suffer with him, that we may be also glorified together. For I reckon that the sufferings of this present time are not worthy to be compared with the glory which shall be revealed in us. For the earnest expectation of the creature waiteth for the manifestation of the sons of God. For the creature was made subject to vanity, not willingly, but by reason of him who hath subjected the same in hope, Because the creature itself also shall be delivered from the bondage of corruption into the glorious liberty of the children of God. For we know that the whole creation groaneth and travaileth in pain together until now. And not only they, but ourselves also, which have the firstfruits of the Spirit, even we ourselves groan within ourselves, waiting for the adoption, to wit, the redemption of our body. For we are saved by hope: but hope that is seen is not hope: for what a man seeth, why doth he yet hope for? But if we hope for that we see not, then do we with patience wait for it. Likewise the Spirit also helpeth our infirmities: for we know not what we should pray for as we ought: but the Spirit itself maketh intercession for us with groanings which cannot be uttered. And he that searcheth the hearts knoweth what is the mind of the Spirit, because he maketh intercession for the saints according to the will of God. And we know that all things work together for good to them that love God, to them who are the called according to his purpose. For whom he did foreknow, he also did predestinate to be conformed to the image of his Son, that he might be the firstborn among many brethren. Moreover whom he did predestinate, them he also called: and whom he called, them he also justified: and whom he justified, them he also glorified. What shall we then say to these things? If God be for us, who can be against us? He that spared not his own Son, but delivered him up for us all, how shall he not with him also freely give us all things? Who shall lay anything to the charge of God's elect? It is God that justifieth. Who is he that condemneth? It is Christ that died, yea rather, that is risen again, who is even at the right hand of God, who also maketh intercession for us. Who shall separate us from the love of Christ? shall tribulation, or distress, or persecution, or famine, or nakedness, or peril, or sword? As it is written, For thy sake we are killed all the day long; we are accounted as sheep for the slaughter. Nay, in all these things we are more than conquerors through him that loved us. For I am persuaded, that neither death, nor life, nor angels, nor principalities, nor powers, nor things present, nor things to come, Nor height, nor depth, nor any other creature, shall be able to separate us from the love of God, which is in Christ Jesus our Lord.

Notes_____

_____

_____

_____

_____

_____

_____

Day Twenty One

DELIGHT YOURSELF IN THE LORD

Fall in love with Jesus and watch how heaven opens up for you. So many people are in love with this world. The Bible tells us that this world is passing away along with all its sinful pleasures. The things in this world might look good and impressive but it's false and not promising. People spend so much time chasing after things and could care less about knowing God Almighty. They do not realize that they are doing things backwards. When you seek after God with all your heart, He will be found by you and in Him, your inheritance abides. The closer you get to God, the more of God you'll desire and the less control this world will have on you. Abide in God and He will abide in you, for without God you can do absolutely nothing. Stop trying to obtain riches and fame, all those things are false and temporary pleasures but God is everlasting. Ask God to help you to see this world for what it is and to help you to love Him more. He knows that you have needs and desires while you are here on earth and does not mind you having things in abundance as long as you don't exchange things for your relationship with Him. Don't make an idol out of things. Keep God on the throne of your life by delighting in Him.

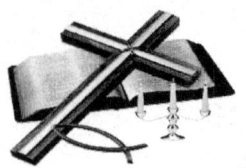

Psalm 37:1-8

Fret not thyself because of evildoers, neither be thou envious against the workers of iniquity. For they shall soon be cut down like the grass, and wither as the green herb. Trust in the LORD, and do good; so shalt thou dwell in the land, and verily thou shalt be fed. Delight thyself also in the LORD: and he shall give thee the desires of thine heart. Commit thy way unto the LORD; trust also in him; and he shall bring it to pass. And he shall bring forth thy righteousness as the light, and thy judgment as the noonday. Rest in the LORD, and wait patiently for him: fret not thyself because of him who prospereth in his way, because of the man who bringeth wicked devices to pass. Cease from anger, and forsake wrath: fret not thyself in any wise to do evil.

Notes_____
_____
_____

Daniel Fast Food List

(You are not limited to these foods. Allow God to lead you on the fast that's best for you)

Vegetables

Artichoke, Asparagus, Beans, Beet, Broccoli, Brussels sprouts, Cabbage, Carrot, Cauliflower, Celeriac, Celery, Chard, Chicory, Collards, Corn, Cress, Cucumbers, Gourds, Jerusalem-Artichoke, Kales, Kohlrabi, Leek, Lettuce, Melons, Mushrooms, Okra, Onions, Parsnips, Peas, Potatoes, Peppers (all kinds), Pumpkins, Radicchio, Radish, Rhubarb, Rutabaga, Shallots, Spinach, Squash, Swede, Sweet-corn, Sweet potato, Tomatoes, Turnips, Watercress, Watermelon, Yams.

Fruit

Acai, Acorn Squash, African Cherry Orange, African Mango, African Mangosteen, Apple, Apricot, Avocado, Banana, Blackberry, Black Mulberry, Blueberry, Brazil Nut, Banana, Butternut Squash, Cherry, Cinnamon Fruit, Citron, Chili Pepper, Clove, Coconut, Cola Nut Fruit, Crabapple, Cranberry, Cucumber, Date, Date Plum, Dragonfruit, Elderberry, Elephant Apple, Fig, Finger Lime, Goji Berry, Golden Apple, Honeyberry, Honeydew Melon, Key Lime, Kiwifruit, Lemon, Lime, Mandarin Orange, Mango, Melon Pear, Miracle Fruit, Noni, Nutmeg, Olive, Orange, Papaya, Passion Fruit, Peach, Peach Palm, Pineapple, Plum, Pomegranate, Pumpkin, Quince, Raspberry, Strawberry, Sycamore Fig, Tangerine, Tomato, Watermelon, Zucchini

Juice

Orange, Grapefruit, Pineapple, Grape,
White-Grape, Pear, Apple, Cranberry, Tomato,
Mango, Pomegranate, Strawberry banana.
Peach, Strawberry raspberry, Cherry,
Carrot juice

Smoothies

Acai Berry, Apples, Bananas,
Blackberries Blueberries, Cherries,
Lemons, Mangos, Melon,
Oranges, Peaches, Peanut
Butter, Pears, Pineapple, Pomegranate, Pumpkin,
Raspberries, Strawberries, Watermelon, Yogurt

Salvation

Romans 10:9-10 says that if thou shalt confess with thy mouth the Lord Jesus, and shalt believe in your heart that God hath raised him from the dead, you shall be saved. For with the heart man believeth unto righteousness; and with the mouth confession is made unto salvation.

If you have not accepted Jesus as Lord and Savior you can do it right now. Just speak out of your mouth these words; "Lord Jesus, I believe that you are the Son of God and that You died on the cross for my sin and God raised You up on the third day for me. I accept You as my Lord and savior, please come into my heart and fill me with Your Holy Spirit". Now you are saved, pray and ask God to lead and guide you to a local church where you can be taught God's word and connect with other believers.

God Bless

Joy K. Blair

Being confident of this very thing, that he which hath begun a good work in you will perform it until the day of Jesus Christ (Philippians 1:6)

"Joy Blair Books where we are making a mark for Jesus one book print at a time"